Ashan Maduranga

Using Bittorent protocol to launch DDoS attacks

GRIN Publishing

Bibliographic information published by the German National Library:

The German National Library lists this publication in the National Bibliography;
detailed bibliographic data are available on the Internet at http://dnb.dnb.de .

Imprint:

Copyright © 2012 GRIN Verlag GmbH
Print and binding: Books on Demand GmbH, Norderstedt Germany
ISBN: 978-3-656-89463-6

This book at GRIN:

http://www.grin.com/en/e-book/289149/using-bittorent-protocol-to-launch-ddos-attacks

GRIN - Your knowledge has value

Since its foundation in 1998, GRIN has specialized in publishing academic texts by students, college teachers and other academics as e-book and printed book. The website www.grin.com is an ideal platform for presenting term papers, final papers, scientific essays, dissertations and specialist books.

Visit us on the internet:

http://www.grin.com/

http://www.facebook.com/grincom

http://www.twitter.com/grin_com

Table of Contents

Table of Figures / Tables

1.0 Title

Enhance security architecture of a BitTorrent client to control DDoS attacks

2.0 Introduction

In a nutshell what the researcher hopes to achieve by this project is to develop a **practical** solution to control Distributed Denial of Service (DDoS) attacks launched using BitTorrent protocol by tweaking the source code of an existing open source BitTorrent client.

Even though BitTorrent is a useful protocol, it could be misused to launch DDoS attacks. Since the number who uses BitTorrent protocol is high, by launching a DDoS the victim's machine could be crippled. Hence as a remedy to the issue this report is formulated so that it discusses how the attacks are done and how it could be prevented.

For a simple analogical demonstration of what this attack does, take a look at figure 1 where computer A cannot fulfill the requests of a legit user computer B. this is what DDoS attack does. After enhancing the security architecture of BitTorrent client this problem would not occur hence it is improved to control these attacks.

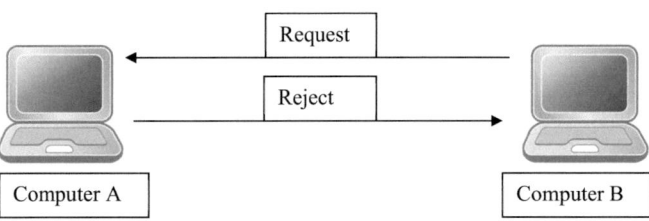

Figure 1 : DDoS analogy

3.0 Problem Statement

In this section the main or the sources of problems related to this project is described in order for the user to understand where and why the idea of this project was originated and how and why it should be eliminated.

3.1 Using BitTorrent protocol to launch DDoS attacks

It has been noted that peer to peer constitute 60% of current internet traffic. (Tsoumakos & Roussopoulos, n.d.) Thus it is apparent that most of the users make use of P2P protocols in a daily basis. If BitTorrent protocol is considered, some of the reasons to choose it over other protocols are its reliability, efficiency and anonymity. (mr6n8, 2012)

3.1.1 How the attack is done

The user should have a meta-data file named ".torrent" to start a torrent service. In this meta-data file, information such as size of each file, hashes for data and IP addresses of trackers[1] are embedded. Hence when the torrent is started, the user checks with the trackers to get a peer list to download pieces of the file he/she needs. (Marlom, et al., 2007) and (Cohen, 2003)

Following table describes various ways that the BitTorrent protocol could be misused to launch DDoS attacks. As seen, it has two modes centralized and DHT mode (which is a current trend to evade the legal actions against torrent and tracker repositories). (Timpanaro, et al., 2011.) However in this report, the second attack method in the table is discussed as it could inflict the most damage using Centralized tracker mode;

Table 1: Different Attack Methods

	Attack Method	BitTorrent Mode	Requirements
1	Report victim as a participating peer	Centralized Tracker Mode	Send a spoofed message to the tracker announcing victim as a participating peer in the swarm (mentioned and implemented in [10]). Or if one of the trackers is compromised, include the victim's address in the peer list.
2	Report victim as a tracker	Centralized Tracker Mode	Publish torrent file with multiple trackers. At least one entry contains the address of the victim. Another entry contains the address of a modified tracker, which replies with a fake number of seeders/leechers
3	Report Victim as Peer in DHT	DHT Mode	Send a spoofed PING message to the DHT, including the victim's source IP (mentioned in [10], but not implemented)
4	Combine 1, 2, 3	both modes	All requirements of 1, 2, 3

Table 1: Different attack methods (Defrawy, et al., 2008)

According to Givanni (2008),*"File sharing protocols such as BitTorrent use centralized server for connections between peers. This procedure create a point of failure because*

---

[1] A tracker is a central element that co-ordinates a swarm and helps peers to find other peers in the same swarm

malicious centralized-server modifies can redirect peer connections toward a target machine on a specific port"

Thus the attacker runs a modified BitTorrent tracker so that the meta-data file has multiple trackers. First tracker respond with fake high statistics to make it appeal for the users to download and the second tracker consist of victims IP address. (Defrawy, et al., 2008).

Hence when the user runs the torrent file, it sends BitTorrent handshakes to the targeted machine in a regular time period. This is very efficient since there is no BitTorrent handshake between the peer and the tracker although such a handshake exists between peers. (Defrawy, et al., 2008).

3.2 The attack is an effective geographically scalable DDoS

As described in the above section P2P is used by many users all around the world. Also the number of users using BitTorrent protocol grows exponentially. (Firas, et al., 2011) The same theory could be applied when it comes to the geography of the users. A study done by Defrawy, K. E., Minas, G. & Athina, M has proven that the average users in a torrent swarm is approximately 20 hops away from where it was published. (Defrawy, et al., 2008) Therefore we could conclude that hundreds and thousands of computers are engage in a DDoS attack expanding the geographical scalability of the attack. (Jerome, et al., n.d.)

3.3 Lack of awareness about this vulnerability among the public

According to Firas, et al., (2011), *"In BitTorrent protocol out-of-hand interaction happens between peers before joining the network"*. This suggests that there are numerous activities that take place in the back end when the user runs the BitTorrent client which the user is not informed of. Hence it is safe to assume that not all of the users are aware of these interactions that occur such as connecting with the tracker, getting the peer list and the functions such as choking, un-choking to download and upload respectively.

According to Givvani, (2008), *"Bit Torrent protocol is an open protocol and today exists many client software implantations used by users. Besides, many users never will upgrade their software client if it works fine in file downloading."* This is also a serious issue and is very common among most of the users. Also the importance of users awareness is highlighted by Mirkovi´c et al., (2002) when he stated *"DDoS attacks should be stopped as close to the sources as possible."* in his article "Attack DDoS at its source". Most of the users are not very attentive of the security side of their BitTorrent client resulting in not updating the security patches that are available to them because as far as the user is concerned, their program works and they are not willing to go through that burden of taking extra measures to ensure cyber security.

4.0 Research aim and Objectives

4.1 Research aim

The main aim of this research is to investigate the security architecture of an existing BitTorrent client and enhance it to control DDoS attacks launched by abusing the BitTorrent protocol in centralized tracker mode.

4.2 Research objectives

- ✓ To investigate in depth on how BitTorrent protocol works.
- ✓ To identify the motives of the attacker and the reason for choosing BitTorrent protocol as the attack method compared to other DDoS attack methods.
- ✓ To investigate in depth on how a particular open source BitTorrent client works with centralized tracker mode. (including the programming language it is build on)
- ✓ To investigate in depth how the attack is carried out using BitTorrent protocol.
- ✓ To investigate how the torrent client could be tweaked to prevent a DDoS attack by identifying malicious trackers and blacklisting them.
- ✓ To investigate the legal, ethics and cyber laws regarding DDoS attacks and its implications.
- ✓ To make sure the BitTorrent clients are up to date with the new security infrastructure. (Examples : by notifying the users of its importance)

5.0 Research Questions

1. Why the attacker would chose BitTorrent protocol handshakes as the preferred method of DDoS attack?
2. What is the time taken to reach a specific threshold in incoming traffic of the victim that could result in a DDoS?
3. What are the current defensive mechanisms used by torrent client, tracker and websites that distribute .torrent file to defend against DDoS attacks?
4. What is a suitable torrent client that could be developed in order to prevent DDoS attacks considering the factors such as programming language and the tracker mode?
5. How to tweak the source code of the selected torrent client to identify and black list the malicious trackers to control DDoS attacks?
6. What are the implications of launching DDoS attacks in the perspective of cyber security and computer ethics?
7. How and what are the ways the updated torrent client be presented to the general public and organizations in real world?
8. What are the difficulties faced by the users and organizations when the updated client is implemented in the real world?

6.0 Research design

In order to collect information to answer the research questions, the researcher basically divides his research into technical and domain sections based on the source of the data and what it covers. Technical research would cover the technical research questions such as number 1, 2, 4, 5 and 6.

In order to complete the technical research questions 1, 2 and 6 the data would be collected by reading the specialized white paper releases on the BitTorrent protocol, its security architecture and the legal implications by referring to materials such as: BotTorrent: Misusing BitTorrent to Launch DDoS Attacks by Minas, G. & Athina, M, A BitTorrent driven distributed denial of service, by Jerome, H., Corey, K. & Cliff, Z. C, and the books named "peer to peer : collaboration and sharing over the internet by bo leuf " and Computer Network Security and Cyber Ethics by Joseph Migga Kizza will be read and studied.

Question numbers 4 and 5 demands to find a suitable open source torrent client to tweak the source code so as to stop DDoS attacks. The source code of a selected client program could be retrieved from sites such as http://sourceforge.net/ and http://osliving.com/ web sites for free. Once downloaded, the programming language it was coded on could be excelled by the author so as to find a solution to question 5.

The domain research (question numbers 1, 3, 6, 7 and 8) would be done by collecting both qualitative and quantitative data collection methods according to judgment sampling. In order to collect qualitative exploratory data, semi-structured interview format would be carried out by interviewing IT security experts such as lecturers of UCTI while abiding to the ethics of researches such as objectivity to avoid biasness. Once the report is done it will be signed by that respective interviewee to ensure honesty, openness, integrity, confidentiality and responsibility publication of facts.

In order to find quantitative data, since the researcher uses judgment sampling people that are surveyed are divided into homogenous groups such as people well versed in technical aspect and normal subjects that uses BitTorrent protocol so that the type of questioners will be different according to their categories.

7.0 Personal reflection

The study aim of this research is to find the ways and means how BitTorrent protocol could be abused to launce DDoS which uses centralized tracker mode. One of the limitations in this study aim is the use of centralized tracker. In current days most of the popular torrent clients such as BitTorrent and UTorrent uses DHT[2] (Distributed Hash Table) which is tracker less to find the blocks and pieces of the files. Observe Table 1: Different attack methods for the different types of attack methods. Another way to do a DDoS attack is by both DHT and central tracker mode to report the victim's source IP as one of the peers.

One of the main drawbacks of reporting victims IP as a peer is that in order to launch the DDoS attack is that the victim should run a BitTorrent client as well. Hence this alternative approach to launch DDoS attack was discarded by the author. Anyhow given that this method is a possibility, then the researcher should find a way to identify the malicious nodes by using behavioral and probabilistic based anomaly detection. (Givanni, 2008). Furthermore researches could be conducted on how the attack is exactly being done, how to prevent it and

---

[2] A method for storing hash tables in geographically distributed locations in order to provide a failsafe lookup mechanism for distributed computing (Inc., 2012)

answers to all the questions listed in the research questions section through books and whitepapers.

Another limitation of this research aim is to find an open source client using a centralized tracker which is very common among users. The researcher has to find a client that is best suitable for the upgrade and if necessary get the consent of the developers for legal purposes if needed.

8.0 References

Cohen, B., 2003. *Incentives Build Robustness in BitTorrent.*

Defrawy, K. E., Minas, G. & Athina, M., 2008. *BotTorrent:Misusin BitTorrent to Launch DDoS Attacks,* Irvine: University of California.

Firas, B., Andra, R. & Hani, R.-H., 2011. *A new security architecture for BitTorrent,* Kent: School of computing University of Kent UK.

Givanni, B., 2008. *A distrubuted denial of service (DDoS) attack using BitTorrent peer-topeer (P2P) network,* Berlin: Technische Universitat Berlin.

Inc., T.C.L.C., 2012. [Online] Available at: http://www.pcmag.com/encyclopedia_term/0,1237,t=DHT&i=41223,00.asp [Accessed 1 July 2012].

Jerome, H., Corey, K. & Cliff, Z. C., n.d. *A BitTorrent driven distributed denial of service,* Orlando: School of Electrical Engineering and Computer Science.

mr6n8, 2012. [Online] Available at: http://www.techsupportalert.com/what-is-bittorrent [Accessed 6 July 2012].

Marlom, K. A., Marinho, B. P. & Rodrigo, M. B., 2007. *Attacking a swarm with a band of liars : evaluating the impact of attacks on BitTorrent,* Sao Leopoldo: UNISINOS.

Mirkovi´c, J., Prier, G. & Reiher, P., 2002. *Attacking DDoS at the Source.* Los Angeles: IEEE Computer Society University of California Los Angeles.

Tsoumakos, D. & Roussopoulos, N., n.d. *Adaptive Probabilistic Search for Peer-to-Peer Networks.* University of Maryland.

Timpanaro, J. P., Cholez, T., Chrisment, I. & Fester, O., 2011. *BitTorrent's mainline DHT security assessment,* Nancy: Henri Poincare University Francy.